Issues today
A resource for KS3

Sport

Editor: **Lisa Firth**

ISSUE
48

Independence
Educational Publishers
Cambridge

First published by Independence

The Studio, High Green, Great Shelford

Cambridge CB22 5EG

England

© Independence 2011

British Library Cataloguing in Publication Data

Sport. – (Issues today ; v. 48)

1. Sports – Social aspects – Juvenile literature.

2. Sports – Moral and ethical aspects – Juvenile literature.

I. Series II. Firth, Lisa.

306.4'83-dc22

ISBN-13: 978 1 86168 581 0

Acknowledgements

The publisher is grateful for permission to reproduce the following material.

While every care has been taken to trace and acknowledge copyright, the publisher tenders its apology for any accidental infringement or where copyright has proved untraceable. The publisher would be pleased to come to a suitable arrangement in any such case with the rightful owner.

Chapter One: Sporting Trends

Taking part in organised sport, © Ipsos MORI, *Investing in inclusive sport,* © Sport England, *2012 to make history as first gender equality Games,* © Sport England, *Sport and gender,* © The British Library Board, *Wheelchair sport FAQs,* © Wheelpower 2010, *Asians in football,* © Kick It Out 2010, *Leagues behind: football's failure to tackle anti-gay abuse,* © Stonewall 2010, *Violence down at football grounds,* © The Football League.

Chapter Two: Good Sportsmanship

Cricket teaches 'Fitness, Friendship and Fair play', © Cricket Foundation Enterprises, *A game of two halves: the politics of football,* © The Learning Skills and Improvement Service 2010, *Sports stars are no role models, say scientists,* © University of Manchester, *The history of drugs in sport,* © TeachPE.com 2010, *Sport cheats are bottom of the class in pupil poll,* © Cricket Foundation Enterprises, *Drug testing in sport,* © TeachPE.com 2010.

All illustrations, including the cover, are by Don Hatcher.

Typesetting by Andrew Young on behalf of Independence.

Additional editorial by Carolyn Kirby on behalf of Independence.

Printed in Great Britain by MWL Print Group Ltd.

Lisa Firth

Cambridge

January 2011

Issues today

Sport

Contents

About Key Stage 3

Key Stage 3 refers to the first three years of secondary schooling, normally years 7, 8 and 9, during which pupils are aged between 11 and 14.

This series is also suitable for Scottish P7, S1 and S2 students.

About *Issues Today*

Issues Today is a series of resource books on contemporary social issues for Key Stage 3 pupils. It is based on the concept behind the popular *Issues* series for 14- to 18-year-olds, also published by Independence.

Each volume contains information from a variety of sources, including government reports and statistics, newspaper and magazine articles, surveys and polls, academic research and literature from charities and lobby groups. The information has been tailored to an 11 to 14 age group; it has been rewritten and presented in a simple, straightforward format to be accessible to Key Stage 3 pupils.

In addition, each *Issues Today* title features handy tasks and assignments based on the information contained in the book, for use in class, for homework or as a revision aid.

Issues Today can be used as a learning resource in a variety of Key Stage 3 subjects, including English, Science, History, Geography, PSHE, Citizenship, Sex and Relationships Education and Religious Education.

About this book

Sport is the forty-eighth volume in the *Issues Today* series. Sport is an important part of our society, from school sports days to major sporting competitions like the Olympic and Paralympic Games. On average, young people in Britain spend just over three hours every week participating in sport, and with London 2012 on the horizon, sport and how it affects our daily lives is receiving more attention than ever before.

This book looks at the issues surrounding sport, including the debates surrounding inclusive sport, the use of performance-enhancing drugs, whether professional athletes are good role models and players' wages.

In addition, at the end of each article is a URL for the relevant organisation's website, which can be visited by pupils who want to carry out further research.

Because the information in this book is gathered from a number of different sources, pupils should think about the origin of the text and critically evaluate the information that is presented. Does the source have a particular bias or agenda? Are you being presented with facts or opinions? Do you agree with the writer?

At the end of each chapter there are two pages of activities relating to the articles and issues raised in that chapter. The 'Brainstorm' questions can be done as a group or individually after reading the articles. This should prompt some ideas and lead on to further activities. Some suggestions for such activities are given under the headings 'Oral', 'Moral Dilemmas', 'Research', 'Written' and 'Design' that follow the 'Brainstorm' questions.

For more information about *Issues Today* and its sister series, *Issues* (for pupils aged 14 to 18), please visit the Independence website.

www.independence.co.uk

Taking part in organised sport

THE DEPARTMENT FOR CHILDREN, SCHOOLS AND FAMILIES commissioned Ipsos MORI in early 2008 to carry out a year-long survey to measure children and young people's participation in out-of-school sporting opportunities and their total participation in sporting opportunities, both in and out of school/college. The questions were asked of 5- to 19-year-olds and the study focuses on two broad age groups: 5- to 16-year-olds in school years Reception to 11, and 16- to 19-year-olds in years 12 and above, or who are not at school. Average findings are reported for the year.

Organised sport outside the school day

The mean level of reported participation in organised sport outside of the school day among 5- to 19-year-olds was just over an hour and a half (97.2 minutes) the week before the interview with the child/young person.

The key findings below are given in terms of the proportion of children and young people who reported participating in at least three hours of organised sport outside of the school day during the week prior to the interview.

► Just over one in five 5- to 19-year-olds (21%) have taken part in three hours or more organised sport. 47% have done no organised sport.

► The proportion of those participating in three hours or more organised sport is the same among 5- to 16-year-olds in years Reception to 11 (21%) and among 16- to 19-year-olds in years 12 or above, or not at school (22%).

► Boys are significantly more likely than girls to have participated in three or more hours (26% vs. 16%). Girls are more likely than boys to have been completely inactive (52% vs. 43%).

► Those 5- to 19-year-olds in the more affluent social groups are more likely than those in less affluent social groups to have participated in three or more hours (24% compared with 18%).

" In both age groups boys were statistically more likely than girls to have participated in at least three hours of physical activity. "

► Young people aged 5 to 19 who have a disability are more likely to be inactive (60%) than those who do not (47%).

► Children and young people aged 5 to 19 from a white ethnic background are more likely than those from a black ethnic background to take part in at least three hours of organised sport (21% and 17%, respectively).

► Looking at Key Stages, those in Key Stages 3, 4 or 5 are more likely to participate in at least three hours than those in Key Stages 1 or 2 (25% compared with 12% and 21%, respectively).

► Of 16- to 19-year-olds, those who are currently in sixth form college (26%) or at school (23%) are significantly more likely to have done at least three hours of organised sport than those in higher education (21%), working (19%) or unemployed (12%).

Total amount of organised sport

A measure of the total time spent participating in organised sport (in and out of school/college) was calculated. The mean level of reported participation among 5- to 19-year-olds in any organised sport in the week before the interview with the child/young person was just under three hours (179.8 minutes).

The key findings below report in terms of the proportion of 5- to 16-year-olds in years Reception to 11 taking part in at least five hours of organised sport a week, and the proportion of 16- to 19-year-olds in years 12 or above or not at school, taking part in at least three hours of organised sport a week.

Taking part in organised sport

For those aged 5 to 16 years old:

- The mean time spent participating in organised sport overall stands at over three hours (197.5 minutes).

- One in five children and young people (22%) aged 5 to 16 have participated in at least five hours of organised sport during and outside the school day in the past week. This comprises any time spent participating either during or outside the school day.

- Boys are more likely to have participated in at least five hours of physical activity than girls (26% vs.18%).

- There are no significant differences by ethnic group.

- Those in the more affluent social groups are more likely to have participated in five hours of organised sport than those in less affluent social groups (25% vs. 20%, respectively).

- Children and young people who have a disability are more likely to have done no organised sport in the last seven days than those who do not (22% have done nothing, compared with 11% of able-bodied children).

- Just under three in ten of those studying at Key Stage 3 or Key Stage 4 level have done at least five hours of sport in the past seven days (27%), but only 19% of those at Key Stage 1 and Key Stage 2 have done the same.

For those aged 16 to 19 years old:

- Just over a quarter (26%) of 16- to 19-year-olds have participated in at least three hours of organised sport during and outside the school/college day.

- The mean time spent participating in organised sport overall stands at just over two hours (125.3 minutes).

- Boys are more likely than girls to have participated in at least three hours of organised sport in total (34% vs. 18%, respectively).

- Young people from the more affluent social groups are more likely than those from less affluent social groups to have done three hours or more organised sport (30% compared with 21%).

- Those who are in school or sixth form college (32%) are more likely than those who are unemployed (12%) to have taken part in three hours of organised sport or more in the past week. Three-quarters (75%) of those who are unemployed have been completely inactive.

- There are no significant differences by ethnic group.

July 2009

> **Just over one in five 5- to 19-year-olds (21%) have taken part in three hours or more organised sport.**

Mini glossary

commissioned – paid someone to carry out a job

affluent – well-off; rich

mean – the average of a set of values

The above information is an edited extract from the omnibus survey Children and Young People's Participation in Organised Sport *produced by Ipsos MORI on behalf of the Department for Children, Schools and Families, and is reprinted with permission. Visit www.dcsf.gov.uk for more information or to view the full text and references.*
© *Ipsos MORI 2009*

www.dcsf.gov.uk

Investing in inclusive sport

SPORT ENGLAND TODAY ANNOUNCED NEW INVESTMENT and a fresh approach to bringing sporting opportunities to disabled people, ensuring the 2012 Paralympic Games deliver a lasting grassroots sporting legacy.

A total of £3.54 million will be available to nine national disability sports organisations, who will now focus on inclusion, integrating the sport on offer to disabled and non-disabled people. Sport England is investing £1.54 million of Exchequer funding in the English Federation of Disability Sport (EFDS), which has announced a new plan to increase participation and opportunities for disabled people, following a major review.

In addition, EFDS and eight other national disability sports organisations have the opportunity to bid for up to £2 million of National Lottery funding. The investment will help these bodies to develop a skilled workforce that can advise, support and guide other sports organisations, as they create opportunities for participation by disabled people.

Sport England's Chief Executive Jennie Price said: 'With only one in 15 disabled adults playing sport regularly – and a decline in that number over the past year – there is a clear need for a change of direction. The investments we are announcing today will create the right environment for increased participation by disabled people.'

Professor David Croisdale-Appleby, the chair of EFDS, said: 'This welcome increase in funding from Sport England will enable EFDS, together with our national member organisations, to implement our new strategy to halt and then reverse the decline in sports participation amongst people with disabilities. It is an exciting development for everyone involved.'

Sport England also confirmed that a further £8 million of National Lottery funding has been assigned for investment in sport for disabled people over the next two years. Sport England is working with the sector to identify specific barriers to disabled participation and how best to target the additional £8-million investment to ensure the best results for sport for disabled people.

Investing in inclusive sport

£2-million of National Lottery investment is available for applications from EFDS and its eight member organisations:

▶ British Amputee and Les Autre Sports Association

▶ British Blind Sport

▶ CP Sport

▶ Mencap Sport

▶ UK Deaf Sport

▶ Wheelpower

▶ Dwarf Athletic Association

▶ Special Olympics

No other organisation is eligible to apply in relation to this funding. Sport England invests National Lottery and Exchequer funding in organisations and projects that will grow and sustain participation in grassroots sport and create opportunities for people to excel at their chosen sport.

Sport England is committed to creating a world-leading community sport system, and has set specific and measurable targets to achieve by 2012/13:

⊘ One million people doing more sport.

⊘ A 25% reduction in the number of 16- to 18-year-olds who drop out of at least five key sports.

⊘ Improved talent development systems in at least 25 sports.

⊘ A measurable increase in people's satisfaction with their experience of sport.

⊘ A major contribution to the delivery of the five-hour sports offer for children and young people.

18 March 2010

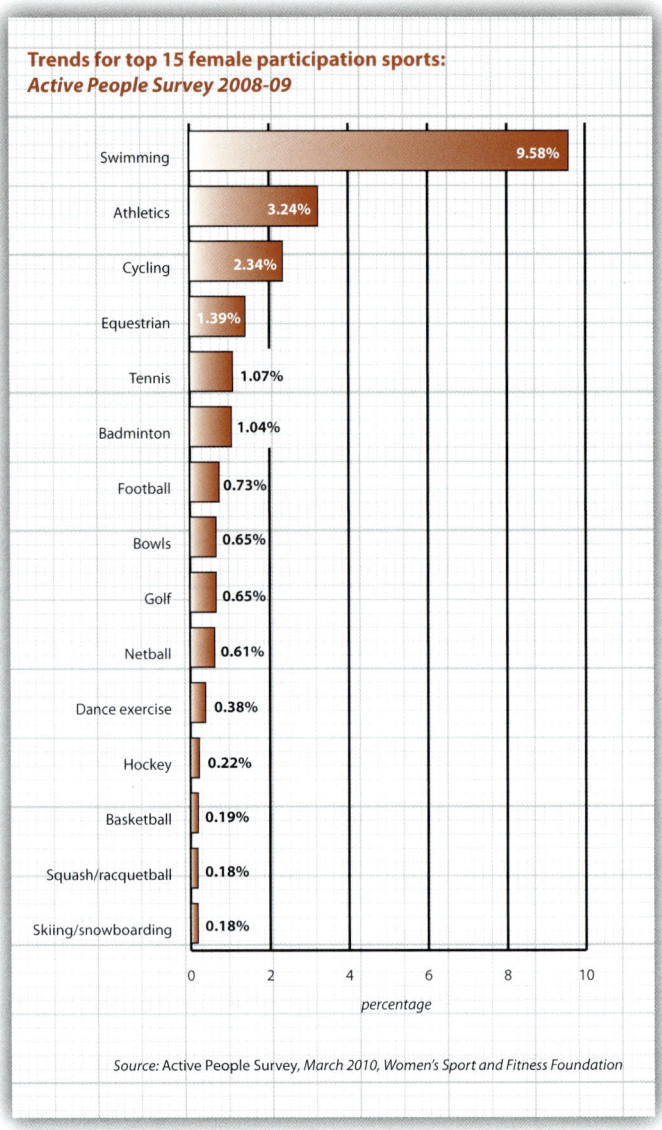

Trends for top 15 female participation sports:
Active People Survey 2008-09

Sport	Percentage
Swimming	9.58%
Athletics	3.24%
Cycling	2.34%
Equestrian	1.39%
Tennis	1.07%
Badminton	1.04%
Football	0.73%
Bowls	0.65%
Golf	0.65%
Netball	0.61%
Dance exercise	0.38%
Hockey	0.22%
Basketball	0.19%
Squash/racquetball	0.18%
Skiing/snowboarding	0.18%

percentage

Source: Active People Survey, March 2010, Women's Sport and Fitness Foundation

 **Sport England is aiming to have one million people doing more sport by 2013.**

Mini glossary

inclusive – something which includes; in which everyone can take part

investment – to have put money into something

grassroots – fundamental; relating to common, everyday people rather than an elite

legacy – something which is handed down to the next generation

www.sportengland.org

2012 to make history as first gender equality Games

LONDON 2012 WILL MAKE HISTORY as first Games to have representation by men and women in every sport.

Sport England has welcomed the IOC's recommendation that women's boxing should be part of the Olympic and Paralympic Games programme.

This means that London 2012 will make history as the first Games to have representation by men and women in every sport.

Back in December, we announced that we would be investing £4.7 million in the Amateur Boxing Association of England (ABAE) to encourage more people to take up the sport – and help talented boxers reach the top. As part of their plan, the ABAE is focusing on women and girls. Particular programmes include:

Increasing participation rates of women and girls by 10%. Initiatives include the setting up of local women's boxing development groups and providing 'summer box camps' for women and girls. The ABAE will also work with Positive Futures on activity programmes, specifically designed for 12- to 19-year-old girls.

Increasing opportunities for women and girls to box (50% of all clubs providing opportunities for women and girls) – By directly supporting their clubs, officials and volunteers, the ABAE will recruit more female boxers and promote 'ready and willing' clubs focused on being more accessible to women.

Removing barriers to participation and tackling misconceptions – By engaging with the 'Make Active Attractive' campaign, the ABAE is going to create more opportunities and pathways for women boxers, providing greater female role models, training more female coaches and boosting the number of women volunteering within the sport by up to 500.

The ABAE has also recently published a guide for women and girls on how to get started in boxing.

Jennie Price, Sport England's Chief Executive, said: 'New Olympic events will bring fresh inspiration and encourage budding sportsmen and women to take up something new. Our role at Sport England is to ensure this is matched by improvements at the grassroots so that people inspired by the Olympics will be able to join, and stay part of, what will be the best community sport system in the world.'

Sue Tibballs, Chief Executive of the Women's Sport and Fitness Foundation, said: 'We are delighted that women's boxing will be at London 2012. With the sport dating back to the 1720s, it's been a long, hard fight to get to today's decision, but we hope it represents a wider move towards gender equality at the Games.'

> ❝ *New Olympic events will bring fresh inspiration and encourage budding sportsmen and women to take up something new.* ❞

Golf and Rugby Union (in the form of Rugby Sevens) have also been recommended for inclusion in the Olympic programme – from 2016 onwards. Final decisions will be made by the IOC membership in October.

Mini glossary

gender equality – *affording the same rights and opportunities to both men and women*

IOC – *International Olympic Committee*

misconceptions – *having an idea or opinion about something before you know the facts about it*

The above information is reprinted with kind permission from Sport England.
© Sport England

www.sportengland.org

Sport and gender

SEX, GENDER AND THE OLYMPICS – *some of the issues.*

Women did not compete in the first modern Olympics of 1896. They started to compete four years later but in only two sports: tennis and golf.

Men have (to date) been excluded from participating in synchronised swimming. Historically, women have been excluded from boxing. 2012 will be the first Olympics in which women have been able to participate in this sport.

Gender equality and the Olympics

There have been a number of cases in which women athletes have been 'accused' of being men pretending to be women, to gain advantage over other women competitors; there is no similar history in the Olympics of women being 'accused' of masquerading as men.

The IOC practised 'gender verification' until 1999.

In 2006 there was one woman on the IOC Executive Board. There were 14 men.

The 2004 IOC Stockholm committee agreed that transsexual athletes could compete in the Olympics, but only after sufficient hormone therapy.

Mini glossary

gender verification – *checking that someone is the gender they claim to be*

transsexual – *someone who identifies as the opposite sex to the one they were born. They may undergo hormone treatment and surgery to attain the characteristics of the sex they identify as*

DID YOU KNOW ?

The London 2012 Olympic Games will be the first opportunity for women to compete in Olympic boxing.

The above information is reprinted with kind permission from The British Library.
© The British Library Board

www.bl.uk

Wheelchair sport FAQs

INFORMATION FROM Wheelpower.

What sports are suitable for people in wheelchairs?

There is a wide range of sports that people in wheelchairs can play. These include sports such as archery, athletics (track and field), wheelchair basketball, bowls, cue sports (snooker and nine-ball pool), wheelchair rugby, wheelchair racing (road), fencing, handcycling, powerlifting, racquetball, swimming, table tennis and tennis.

There are also a number of other newer sports like wheelchair badminton and winter sports including wheelchair curling, ice sledge hockey and skiing, where people use specially designed equipment to participate.

Nowadays, there is a wide range of other activities available for recreational sport and fitness, and contacts for many of these activities can be found on the WheelPower website (www.wheelpower.org.uk).

Do you need a special chair to play wheelchair sport?

Although at entry level it is not essential to have a specialised sports wheelchair, many of the sports use equipment and chairs to make them easier to play and a sports wheelchair can make a big difference to someone's enjoyment of a sport.

Manufacturers of sports wheelchairs include Invacare, RGK, Bromakin, Draft, Da Vinci and Quickie.

WheelPower provides funding for manual sports wheelchairs through our Wheel Appeal scheme: application forms and criteria are available on our website.

Sports wheelchairs are very personal and are available from a number of manufacturers and suppliers.

At junior level there are some organisations who do help with funding, including The Lords Taverners, Get Kids Going, Variety Club Easy Riders and Whizz-Kidz.

What are the Paralympic Games?

Held in 'parallel' with the winter and summer Olympic Games, the Paralympic Games are the 'Olympics for the disabled'. Held in the same city and year as the Olympics, the Paralympic Games are the ultimate sporting challenge for a disabled sportsman or woman.

In 2010 the Winter Paralympic Games were held in Vancouver, Canada, from 12-21 March and in 2012 the twelfth Summer Paralympic Games will be held in London, UK, from 29 August-9 September and will include some 5,000 athletes from around 150 countries.

How do I start playing wheelchair sport?

Depending on someone's age they could start at a number of WheelPower events.

- Primary Sports Camps are one-day fun sports camps introducing sport to 6- to 11-year-old children with disabilities.

- Junior Sports Camps are one-/two-day camps providing coaching and sport to 11- to 18-year-old children with disabilities.

- National Junior Games for 11- to 18-year-olds offer a combination of coaching and competition.

- Sports Camps – organised by the Our Sports Associations who are partners with WheelPower, for adults and children at all levels from introduction to elite. These camps are usually over the weekend and many take place at the Stoke Mandeville Stadium.

- Sport for all – many are held annually at the Stoke Mandeville Stadium by sports associations supported by WheelPower, in around six different sports. Although they are championships they also include many athletes at intermediate level and offer competition in different sports and classes.

Wheelchair sport FAQs

How is wheelchair sport funded?

WheelPower is the national charity for wheelchair sport in the UK. Funded through donations and contributions from charitable trusts, groups and individuals, the charity annually tries to raise around £1 million to fund its work in providing sporting opportunities for disabled people.

Who was Ludwig Guttmann?

The late Sir Ludwig Guttmann was the founder of WheelPower and sport for the disabled. Guttmann, a German neurologist, set up the National Spinal Injuries Centre at Stoke Mandeville Hospital in the late 1940s and introduced sport as part of the rehabilitation of his patients.

In 1948 he organised the first national competition to coincide with the London Olympic Games and in 1952 the first international events were organised at Stoke Mandeville. In 1960 the first Paralympic Games were held in Rome and the Pope called Guttmann 'the de Cubertan of the paralysed'.

Guttmann once said: 'If I ever did one good thing in my medical career it was to introduce sport into the rehabilitation of people with disabilities.'

The work Guttmann started has now developed into a Paralympic movement worldwide and he is acknowledged as the father of the Paralympics and sport for the disabled.

What is classification?

Sport is divided into classifications: for example, men compete separately to women; in combat sports, people compete by body weight.

In disabled sport, classification is the method by which fair competition is achieved. In addition to the traditional classifications as above (such as gender), there are classifications based on disability and function.

The systems vary from sport to sport and more recently classification in many sports has been based on functional ability. This has enabled groups to be combined, thereby reducing the number of classifications and improving the competition.

At entry level, classification is usually more important in terms of 'minimum disability'. This is the term used to describe the minimum level of injury/disability that means someone is allowed to participate in disabled sport.

How should you choose a sport?

Choosing a sport should be based on a few basic principles:

▶ Which sport attracts you.

▶ Which sport you will enjoy the most.

▶ Which sport you are most suited for (physically and technically).

▶ Whether you want to play for fun or in serious competition.

Once you have decided on a sport, give it a try. If you find it's not for you there are many others to choose from and you may find you are better suited to one sport than another.

Some sports are more competitively structured and others offer more social opportunities. All are open to men and women, although some do have age restrictions for participation so it's worth checking first.

Before taking part in any activity it is always worth checking with your doctor to make sure that taking part will not cause you any harm.

Wheelchair sport FAQs

Do wheelchair athletes receive much funding to help them reach elite levels in their sports?

As funding permits, WheelPower supports the participation of British wheelchair athletes in international competition. However, in more recent years support for elite wheelchair athletes has formed part of the World Class Performance funding supported by UK Sport and the National Lottery.

Around how many wheelchair athletes participate in the Paralympic Games?

This varies depending on the number of sports and the number who gain the standards needed to qualify. The GB Team is co-ordinated by ParalympicsGB.

On average, how much publicity does disability sport receive in a year?

Not as much as we would like! Coverage has improved and certain publications like the *Daily Telegraph* and BBC Sport are committed to covering disability sport and the Paralympic Games. Coverage tends to be focused around events and personalities. Channel 4 recently won the rights to cover the 2012 Paralympic Games in London.

> ❝ *In disabled sport, classification is the method by which fair competition is achieved...there are classifications based on disability and function.* ❞

Do you think that wheelchair athletes are treated as fairly as non-wheelchair athletes?

As awareness of wheelchair and Paralympic sport grows and facilities become more accessible then it can be expected that people with disabilities in society will be treated more fairly. Sport is challenging and disabled sport cannot hope to compete with football, rugby and cricket, as the numbers who participate are much smaller.

It is our goal to ensure that our athletes are respected for their abilities and promoted for their achievements. WheelPower tries to ensure that there are the opportunities on offer for all who wish to take part, whether for fun or in serious competition. In order to do this WheelPower needs funding, much of which we raise through charitable donations, fundraising events and with the help of many individuals and volunteers.

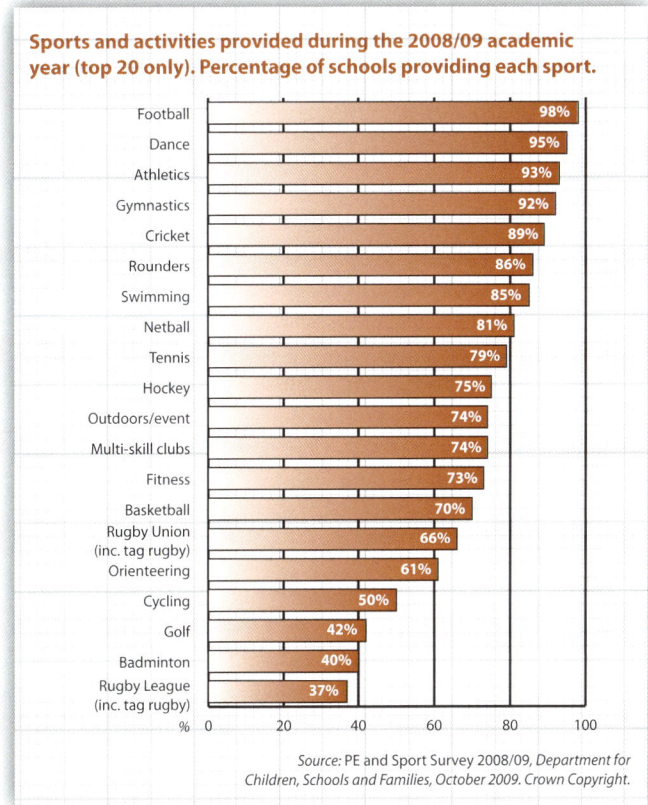

Sports and activities provided during the 2008/09 academic year (top 20 only). Percentage of schools providing each sport.

Sport	Percentage
Football	98%
Dance	95%
Athletics	93%
Gymnastics	92%
Cricket	89%
Rounders	86%
Swimming	85%
Netball	81%
Tennis	79%
Hockey	75%
Outdoors/event	74%
Multi-skill clubs	74%
Fitness	73%
Basketball	70%
Rugby Union (inc. tag rugby)	66%
Orienteering	61%
Cycling	50%
Golf	42%
Badminton	40%
Rugby League (inc. tag rugby)	37%

Source: PE and Sport Survey 2008/09, Department for Children, Schools and Families, October 2009. Crown Copyright.

Mini glossary

rehabilitation – *helping someone to recover over a long period of time; enabling them to cope with their disability*

The above information is reprinted with kind permission from WheelPower.
© Wheelpower 2010

www.wheelpower.org.uk

Asians in football

HUNDREDS OF THOUSANDS OF YOUNG ASIANS are playing and watching the game around the country every weekend.

But there is a massive under-representation of the Asian community in the professional game. The facts speak for themselves. There are only seven British Asian players in professional football and two major reports from the Asians in Football forum, a decade apart (*Asians Can't Play Football* in 1996 and *Asians Can Play Football* in 2005) have shown little change in Asian representation on the footballing landscape. Within the Asian community there continues to be a feeling that Asian players have been marginalised by the game for far too long. Kick It Out, football's equality and inclusion campaign, has been at the forefront of this cause for over a decade and continues to work to develop football in these communities.

Popular myths

Popular myths such as Asians are only interested in cricket and hockey, that Asians aren't strong enough to play the game professionally and that cultural differences will prevent Asian players developing in football are just a few of the common falsehoods that have prevented Asian players breaking through. In response, a number of groups have organised themselves to ensure they are providing young talented players from the Asian community with the chance to improve and progress.

Teams such as London APSA and Sporting Bengal became the first Asian clubs to play in the FA Cup in 2005. Albion Sports Club from Bradford, perhaps Britain's most successful local Asian Football Club, have reached the nationwide FA Sunday Cup Final twice, Elite Youth of East London has grown to become part of the well organised and funded Osmani Trust and the London Asian Football League continues to grow, attracting teams from all backgrounds. These are just a few examples of how Asians are climbing the football ladder.

Trailblazers

While frustrations remain, the love for the game drives on talented young Asians in hoping to achieve the goal of joining trailblazers Zesh Rehman, Michael Chopra and Anwar Uddin in the professional game. Under-representation in other areas of the game is also beginning to be challenged with the successes of Football League referee Mo Matadar, female referee Lisa Rashid and FA Council member Thura Win. The game recognised the need to ensure that the Asian community is no longer excluded from the game following the launch of the *Asians Can Play Football* report in 2005 and the more recent FA working group on Asian Muslim women and girls in football.

Football family commitment

On the recent Asian Soccer Star initiative at Chelsea FC, former Chelsea and England star Graeme Le Saux said, 'We realise that there is a lack of representation of players from Asian backgrounds within the game and we hope that the competition will help inspire Asian youngsters.' He added, 'We want to show that race is no barrier to joining our club and that opportunities for Asian players do exist. We are proud of the religious and racial diversity at Chelsea and it is important that all clubs share our ambition that players should only be judged on their talent and their potential.'

The FA's Simon Johnson said on behalf of the football family: 'We want to create more and better coaches from the Asian communities. We want to create clear pathways for the most talented to progress. We want to ensure that, when the Clubs are scouting for players, they are doing so in such a way that they can find the very best talent from the Asian communities. Each of the bodies has a role to play in making all this happen. We know that, and we are taking the necessary action. We also want to see the active fan base at our clubs adapt to reflect the diversity of the communities in which they play.'

Mini glossary

marginalised – to make less important; to be on the fringes of society

www.kickitout.org

Leagues behind: football's failure to tackle anti-gay abuse

FOOTBALL IS BRITAIN'S NATIONAL GAME. Yet in 2009 not one gay professional footballer in Britain, of which there are undoubtedly many, feels that football is an industry in which it is safe to be openly gay. Neither does the game give lesbian, gay and bisexual football fans and players the respect and protection they deserve.

This research by Stonewall, including a YouGov survey of 2,005 football fans and interviews with football insiders, shows clearly that anti-gay abuse is all too common on both terraces and pitches. This abuse almost always goes unchallenged. Fans believe that it is this abuse, from fans, players and team-mates, that stops gay people from playing football and creates a culture of fear where gay players feel it is unsafe to come out. The research also demonstrates that many others – including women supporters and those with families – are put off attending games by the presence of anti-gay abuse.

Fans are clear that it is the lack of any visible action by the Football Association, football clubs and their partners in tackling anti-gay abuse which has allowed it to continue on the terraces and in changing rooms across Britain. Football fans are also sure that they want this to change and believe that football would be a far better sport if anti-gay abuse was stopped.

Football has had demonstrable success in challenging other problems, from racism to hooliganism. The same high-profile commitment and imagination urgently needs to be applied to tackling anti-gay abuse too. This research provides the Football Association, football clubs and their partners with a clear challenge from fans. If they fail to rise to it, football risks preventing a new generation of talent and losing its right to claim to be Britain's national game for the twenty-first century.

> **Many football fans and individuals working within the football industry believe that the sport is anti-gay. 99**

Summary and key findings

- Many football fans and individuals working within the football industry believe that the sport is anti-gay.

- The majority of fans attending matches have heard homophobic abuse on the terraces.

- Three in four fans think there are gay players currently in the Premier League or Championship.

- Seven in ten think there are gay players in Leagues One or Two.

- Two-thirds of fans would feel comfortable if a player on their team came out but only one in eight think there is a gay player on their team.

- Seven in ten fans who have attended a match in the last five years have heard anti-gay language and abuse on the terraces.

- Three in five fans believe anti-gay abuse from fans prevents gay professional players from coming out.

- One in four believe anti-gay abuse from team-mates contributes to there currently being no openly gay players.

- Over half of football fans think the Football Association, the Premier League and the Football League are not doing enough to tackle anti-gay abuse. Only three in ten believe they are doing enough already.

- Half of football fans think football clubs themselves are not doing enough to tackle anti-gay abuse. Only a third believe they are doing enough already.

- More than one in four football fans think professional football is 'anti-gay'.

- Only one in three fans think football is less anti-gay than 20 years ago.

Leagues behind: football's failure to tackle anti-gay abuse

Fans and individuals working within the football industry are clear that they want football clubs, the Football Association and their partners to demonstrate leadership and make football a better sport by tackling anti-gay abuse. Many feel, however, that to date not enough has been done to tackle anti-gay abuse.

▶ Almost two-thirds of fans believe football would be a better sport if anti-gay abuse and discrimination was stopped.

▶ Only one in six fans say their club is doing work to tackle anti-gay abuse.

▶ Five out of six fans support the police's decision to charge fans with chanting anti-gay and racist abuse at Sol Campbell at the Tottenham Hotspur v Portsmouth game on 28 September 2008.

The benefits for football clubs and football as a whole of tackling anti-gay abuse are clear. Fans would be more likely to attend matches, purchase merchandise and participate in amateur football if anti-gay abuse was tackled.

Two in five lesbian, gay and bisexual fans would be more likely to buy merchandise or tickets if football was more gay-friendly. One in six of all fans would be more likely to attend football matches if anti-gay abuse was tackled.

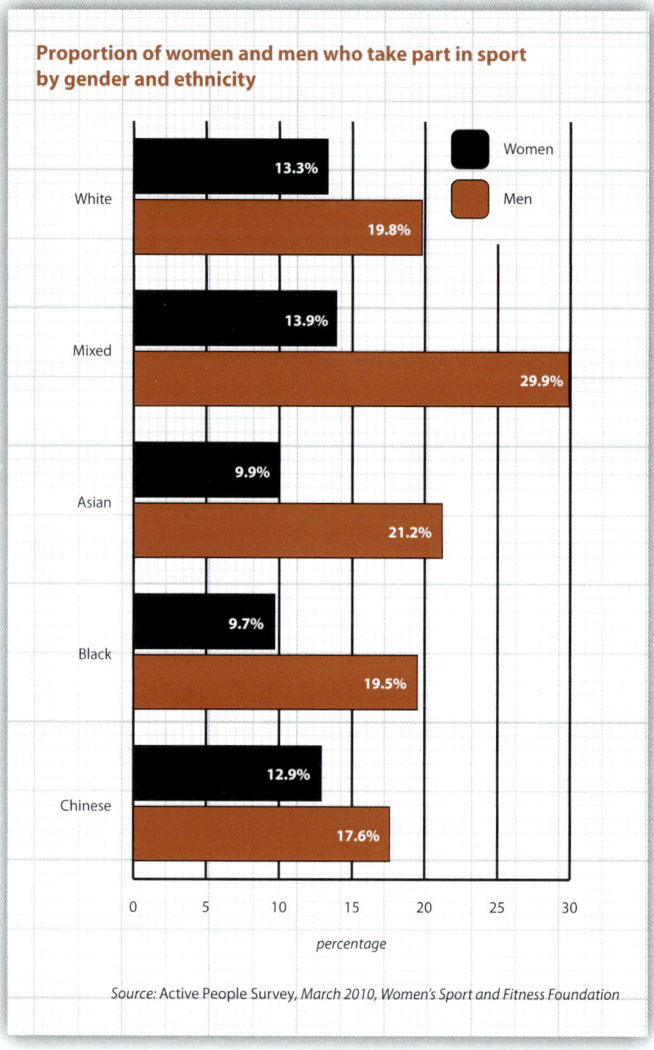

Proportion of women and men who take part in sport by gender and ethnicity

(Women, Men)

Ethnicity	Women	Men
White	13.3%	19.8%
Mixed	13.9%	29.9%
Asian	9.9%	21.2%
Black	9.7%	19.5%
Chinese	12.9%	17.6%

percentage

Source: Active People Survey, *March 2010, Women's Sport and Fitness Foundation*

> 66 Nothing is done to stop homophobic chants. It must be the only profession where the workers feel unable to come out and be accepted for playing football, not what they are. 99

Simon, Ipswich Town supporter

> 66 *Two in five lesbian, gay and bisexual fans would be more likely to buy merchandise or tickets if football was more gay-friendly.* 99

> 66 I think there's still an awful lot to do before anyone's going to come out at the top end of the game, an awful lot. 99

Football industry executive

Mini glossary

terraces – the area in a football stadium where fans stand to watch the match

homophobia – fear or intolerance directed at lesbian and gay people

The above information is an extract from Stonewall's report Leagues Behind: Football's failure to tackle anti-gay abuse, *and is reprinted with permission.* © Stonewall 2010

www.stonewall.org.uk

Violence down at football grounds

ARRESTS FOR VIOLENCE AT FOOTBALL GROUNDS dropped last season, the Home Office Minister David Hanson announced today.

The number of fans arrested overall also fell last year, with no arrests at 67 per cent of all international and domestic matches.

Statistics on Football-Related Arrests and Banning Orders Season 2008-09, published today, revealed there were 3,752 arrests last season – down two per cent on the year before.

They also showed violent incidents were down five per cent, with just 354 fans arrested for violence out of the total attendance figure of 37 million at football matches last year.

Policing Minister David Hanson said: 'Hooligans once blighted our national game, but we now set an example for the rest of the world in how we police football matches.

'I am pleased with the way clubs and police work together, but we must also praise fans for realising violence has no place in the modern game.

'We are not complacent and will carry on working to ensure this success story continues into the future.'

The new figures mean just 0.01 per cent of 37 million supporters attending matches in England and Wales last year were arrested. Fans were also well-behaved abroad – more than 105,000 fans travelled to 49 games in European club competitions last year, but just 30 were arrested.

> **We are not complacent and will carry on working to ensure this success story continues into the future.**

> **More than 105,000 fans travelled to 49 games in European club competitions last year, but just 30 were arrested.**

The latest statistics revealed during the 2008/09 season:

- 3,752 arrests were made at domestic and international matches in England and Wales;

- there were 1.18 arrests per game;

- the number of football banning orders on 10 November was 3,180 – representing 956 new orders imposed last year;

- 92 per cent of individuals whose banning orders have expired are assessed by police as no longer posing a risk to football disorder.

23 December 2009

Mini glossary

blighted – marred; spoiled

www.football-league.co.uk

Activities

Brainstorm

Brainstorm to find out what you know about sport.

1. What reasons are there for getting involved in organised sport?

....

....

2. What sporting activities and events can you name?

....

....

3. What is inclusive sport?

....

....

Oral activities

4. Read *Asians in football* on page 10. Imagine you run a community football team for girls aged 8-12 which has several Asian players. You have more children from a number of different backgrounds on your waiting list but don't have the funding to take them on. Create a PowerPoint presentation pitched at local businesses, encouraging them to sponsor the team and provide additional funding.

NOTES ....

....

5. 'This house believes it should not be compulsory for pupils to take part in organised sport at school.' Debate this motion in two groups, with one group arguing in favour and the other against.

NOTES ....

....

Moral dilemmas

6. Imagine you are attending a football match. During the game, the men next to you start a homophobic chant aimed at the other team's players. One of the men has his young children with him. Would you report the group of fans to the club?

7. Read *Investing in inclusive sport* on pages 3-4. During the recession, organisations offering funding face many competing demands. If you were a member of Sport England faced with the task of deciding how to allocate your funding, what factors would you consider? Do yo think you would vote in favour of making £3.54 million available to disability sports organisations?

Activities

Research activities

8. Read *Violence down at football grounds* on page 13. Use the Internet to research the problem of so-called football 'hooliganism' in 1970s and 80s Britain. Why was football violence such a big problem during these decades? How did measures against hooliganism lead to the Hillsborough tragedy in 1989? How and why have things changed? Write a summary of your findings.

CONCLUSIONS..

....

....

....

....

9. Find out about the South African runner Caster Semenya and the questions raised about her gender following her 800 metres Gold medal win in 2009. How was this handled? Do you think Ms Semenya was treated fairly? Write a summary of your views on the case.

NOTES...

....

....

....

....

Written activities

Complete the following activity in your exercise books or on a sheet of paper.

10. In Olympic and Paralmypic sporting competitions, what is 'classification' and how does it work? Write an article explaining how classifications are decided and why, using information from *Issues Today: Sport* and your own research.

Design activities

11. Design a poster which could be displayed around football stadiums designed to challenge racist or homophobic abuse among fans.

12. Find out about a less well-known Olympic or Paralympic sport and create a flyer aimed at young people, encouraging them to get involved.

Cricket teaches 'Fitness, Friendship and Fair play'

CRICKET IS IMPROVING THE SOCIAL WELLBEING OF THOUSANDS of state school pupils, *according to new research.*

The report by the Institute of Youth Sport (IYS) found that pupils involved in the Chance to Shine initiative showed increased fitness levels, greater social skills and improved sportsmanlike behaviour.

There is also evidence that cricket is improving the behaviour of young people both on and off the sports field, particularly in deprived areas; while the so-called 'gentleman's game' is helping girls to 'overcome restrictive gender beliefs' and gain confidence in playing sport.

It may be helping to cut down truancy, too, as significantly more pupils look forward to and enjoy attending school when Chance to Shine is taking place – 53% – compared to 36% when it is not.

Chance to Shine is the Cricket Foundation's campaign to bring cricket and its educational benefits to at least two million children by 2015. The cricket charity commissioned the IYS, part of Loughborough University, to look at the impact that Chance to Shine had on the 3,000 state schools and 350,000 pupils that took part in 2009.

One of the cricket coaches quoted in the report gave an example of how cricket can support young people in developing friendships and support networks. He described how a child had been severely bullied all his life to the extent that he was 'quite psychologically damaged' and required a psychiatrist. It was only when the child joined the local cricket club, through Chance to Shine, that he started to make friends. His doctor said that 'cricket had been his saviour'.

The research describes how the cricket sessions have contributed positively to the development of pupils' social skills, like teamwork, as one Year 5 pupil explains: 'We've all, like, bonded a bit more. We've realised that we've got to work as a team...because there's no point in just trying to be selfish and barging other people and catching the ball so you get all the pride, but if someone catches it's the whole team's pride.'

Fitness

The Institute of Youth Sport report found that Chance to Shine was having an impact on pupils' fitness levels as they were continually involved and active in various activities throughout the sessions. It also improved pupils' involvement in PE and increased their motivation, especially those that tended to dislike sports, giving them 'a new lease of life' and 'an opportunity to be successful'.

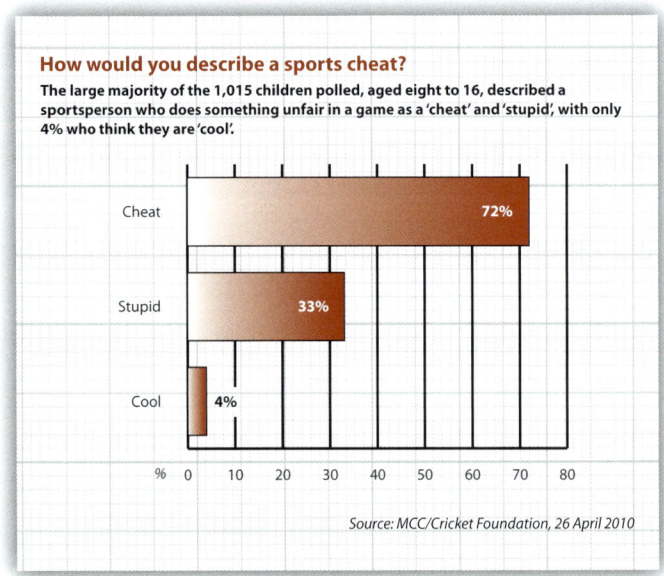

How would you describe a sports cheat?
The large majority of the 1,015 children polled, aged eight to 16, described a sportsperson who does something unfair in a game as a 'cheat' and 'stupid', with only 4% who think they are 'cool'.

Cheat — 72%
Stupid — 33%
Cool — 4%

% 0 10 20 30 40 50 60 70 80

Source: MCC/Cricket Foundation, 26 April 2010

> 66 *Cricket sessions have been effective for reducing 'disruptive behaviour during class and encouraging pupils to act more responsibly.* 99

Cricket teaches 'Fitness, Friendship and Fair play'

Fair play

'Fair play' was a reoccurring theme in the report, with pupils saying that winning is not the most important thing when playing cricket and that they just enjoy participating in cricket as it is 'fun'.

'You learn sportsmanship, you can work together and help people out,' says one Year 5 pupil; while a Year 6 female pupil interviewed says that cheating in cricket was uncommon: 'With football they [the boys] sometimes kick you and things but with cricket no one really tries to trick you and cheat. And we clap when someone does well.'

Earlier this year the charity teamed up with Marylebone Cricket Club, guardian of the Laws and Spirit of Cricket, for a nationwide drive to encourage fair play by introducing a two-hour 'MCC Spirit of Cricket' session to 3,000 state schools during the summer term.

Teachers highlighted how taking part in the programme has encouraged positive changes in pupils in the classroom.

They say the cricket sessions have been effective for reducing disruptive behaviour during class and encouraging pupils to act more responsibly.

'For children with behaviour difficulties, you know they're wanting to turn themselves around,' says one teacher in the report, '...and we take them out of school and I know that I can trust their behaviour within those situations to play the cricket matches...a lot of our best players are the ones who do have some behavioural difficulties.'

Confidence

The value of the cricket sessions for improving girls' confidence was notable and they were especially successful at encouraging Asian girls to become involved in cricket.

Chance to Shine has even helped some girls to gain a new-found status in school: 'It's like everyone says girls can't play cricket, they are no good at boys' sports, but we are doing it and we are really good. We keep winning all the time and it has made the boys realise we can be as good as them.' (Year 6 pupil)

One 13-year-old, Caitlin Byrne from Durham, had never played cricket before Chance to Shine arrived at her school. She discovered she was good at left-arm seam bowling (a cricket bowling technique), a skill which she developed further at South Shields Cricket Club, and she now plays at her age group for Durham County.

Wasim Khan, Chief Executive of the Cricket Foundation, says: 'The news that Chance to Shine is having a major impact on our schools, teachers and pupils is fantastic. We will continue to strive to give as many young people as possible the opportunity to play and be educated through cricket.'

Ashes hero and Chance to Shine Ambassador Andrew Flintoff adds: 'I think it's massively important for kids to get involved in cricket for a number of reasons. First and foremost, it's a lot of fun. But it can also teach you a lot of good things – respect, self-confidence, discipline, all things you need to grow up as a good person.'

8 September 2009

Mini glossary

truancy – *missing school without a valid reason or authorisation from teachers*

www.chancetoshine.org

A game of two halves: the politics of football

THE WORLD OF PROFESSIONAL FOOTBALL is always in the headlines. Premier League footballers and their wives and girlfriends ('WAGs') are a key feature of Britain's celebrity culture. The World Cup and Champions League raise vast sums of money through the sale of TV rights, image rights, replica shirts and ticket sales. On an international level, the choice of nations, by FIFA, to host the World Cup has enormous social, economic and political effects. In spite of the undoubted success of the sport in the era of all-seater stadia and the decrease in the levels of hooliganism witnessed in the 1970s and 1980s, there remain a number of important issues.

Issues in football

During the 2009-10 season the financial collapse of Portsmouth with four owners and debts of £138 million highlighted the rotten state of many clubs' financial position. Outside of the top half of the Premier League many clubs are faced with rising costs, mainly in the form of players' wages, and increasing debts. The way the free market works has allowed investors to borrow huge sums of money to buy clubs and then saddle the club with the debts.

This has happened most notably to Manchester United and Liverpool. In the face of the rich and powerful owners, football supporters' trusts have tried to make their voices heard. In the 2010 General Election both Labour and Conservative manifestos referred to co-operative ownership to give fans a greater say.

The famous Bosman ruling by the European Court enabled players to leave for no transfer fee at the end of their contract and prevented countries from imposing quotas, which would have limited the numbers of foreign players in their teams. The effect was rapid wage inflation and a decline in home-grown talent in British clubs. Top footballers are now more likely to live in gated communities than in the streets where they grew up, which was often the case before the 1960s.

Football is part of society, not separate from it, and it has often highlighted underlying problems in society. In particular, the numbers of black and foreign players entering the game in recent years raised the issue of racism. Anti-racism campaigns have been a feature of the work in all clubs, and action to counter homophobia and sectarianism has also been important.

The question of civil liberties and concerns about the 'surveillance society' are also highlighted in the experience of fans attending football matches. The controversial police practice of 'kettling' (the formation of barriers of police officers to contain a crowd) was developed on football fans, and punishments given out to fans have been criticised as infringing human rights.

YOUR WIFE RANG SIR, APPARENTLY SHE WANTS A TRANSFER!

A game of two halves: the politics of football

£100,000 per week

The list below shows the top 20 earners in world football in 2010. Even below this very top level of football stars, Premiership players all earn between £1 million and £5 million per year. A BBC survey in 2006 showed that age and playing position also made a difference to earnings. Strikers earned the most, then midfielders, then defenders, with goalkeepers earning the least.

Championship players earned about a third of Premiership players' salaries and League One players earned a third of Championship players' wages. League Two players still earned an average of £49,000 in 2006. Highest earnings were made by players aged from 27-30.

World football top earners 2010

1. Cristiano Ronaldo (Real Madrid, £11.3 million)
2. Zlatan Ibrahimovic (Barcelona, £10.4 million)
3. Lionel Messi (Barcelona, £9.1 million)
4. Samuel Eto'o (Internazionale, £9.1 million)
5. Kaka (Real Madrid, £8.7 million)
6. Emmanuel Adebayor (Manchester City, £7.4 million)
7. Karim Benzema (Real Madrid, £7.4 million)
8. Carlos Tevez (Manchester City, £7 million)
9. John Terry (Chelsea, £6.5 million)
10. Frank Lampard (Chelsea, £6.5 million)
11. Thierry Henry (Barcelona, £6.5 million)
12. Xavi (Barcelona, £6.5 million)
13. Ronaldinho (AC Milan, £6.5 million)
14. Steven Gerrard (Liverpool, £6.5 million)
15. Daniel Alves (Barcelona, £6.1 million)
16. Michael Ballack (Chelsea, £5.6 million)
17. Raul (Real Madrid, £5.6 million)
18. Rio Ferdinand (Manchester United, £5.6 million)
19. Kolo Toure (Manchester City, £5.6 million)
20. Wayne Rooney (Manchester United, £5.2 million)

(Source: http:// thetotalfootballer.com)

> **Top footballers are now more likely to live in gated communities than in the streets where they grew up.**

DID YOU KNOW? A Fabian Society/YouGov survey showed that people in Britain think that a fair average salary for a professional footballer would be £62,000 per year.

A game of two halves: the politics of football

Wage cap

One possible solution to the problem of players' ever-rising pay demands is to have wage caps. Some clubs are paying 85 per cent of their income out in players' wages. The result is that in the end they make losses and are effectively bankrupt. A wage-capping scheme has been successfully introduced in League Two. Here clubs must keep players' wages to 60 per cent of their income. Some people think it is a matter of time before all professional clubs introduce similar caps. A similar scheme introduced in Rugby Union saw many top players move to French clubs where they could earn more money as there was no wage cap in France. Below are debate arguments for and against introducing a wage cap.

Arguments for wage capping

▶ It is obscene that a man kicking a ball can earn as much in a week as a doctor dedicated to saving lives can earn in a year.

▶ Huge salaries for players highlight the inequalities in our society and create a massive gap between players and fans.

▶ Top clubs need help to put into practice a cap in the face of growing player power.

▶ Wage caps for clubs would prevent one or two sides buying up all the best talent. More of the money currently pouring into the pockets of a few highly-paid individuals would filter down to the grass roots of the game.

▶ Clubs are being forced to take big risks – gambling future success against increased losses.

▶ Some clubs spend more than 80 per cent of their income on wages and are still relegated.

▶ Owners and managers buy players they cannot afford and put the club into serious debt.

▶ Without wage caps more and more clubs will go bust.

The above information is reprinted with kind permission from the Learning and Skills Improvement Service.
© The Learning Skills and Improvement Service 2010

www.excellencegateway.org.uk

Arguments against wage capping

▶ Footballers have a very short working life – 18 to 35 if they're lucky – and need to maximise their earnings for future years.

▶ Footballers actually earn far less than some other sportsmen, such as Grand Prix drivers, boxers and baseball stars.

▶ Top players are as much entertainers as Hollywood actors and actresses, who can earn millions for just a few months of filming.

▶ Top players earn as much, if not more, as their salaries for their club in ticket sales, merchandise sales and brand marketing.

▶ Supply and demand. In a free market economy, why shouldn't players demand as much as clubs are prepared to pay? If the market collapses, wages will soon decrease – as happened in snooker.

▶ Wage caps would just complicate matters further as clubs would seek to bend the rules using bonuses and secret offshore payments.

▶ A percentage cap is not fair, as the clubs with the highest incomes would still be able to pay the highest wages.

▶ The English game would suffer as the best players could move to Spain or Italy to earn more money.

Mini glossary

era – *a specific period of time*

quota – *a set amount that must not be exceeded*

sectarianism – *being part of a group; showing intolerance or bigotry towards members of other groups*

surveillance society – *this term refers to the idea that our society and individuals within it are constantly monitored*

Sports stars are no role models, say scientists

THE LOUTISH AND DRUNKEN BEHAVIOUR of some of our sporting heroes – often reported in the media – has little or no effect on the drinking habits of young people, new research has found.

Researchers at the Universities of Manchester, UK, and Western Sydney, Australia, say their findings – published in *Drug and Alcohol Review* – disprove the idea that sports stars act as role models for those who follow sport.

'The perceived drinking habits of sports stars and its relationship to the drinking levels of young people has never been examined empirically, despite these sporting heroes often being thought of as influential role models for young people,' said lead researcher Dr Kerry O'Brien, a lecturer in Manchester's School of Psychological Sciences.

'Our research shows that young people, both sporting participants and non-sporting participants, don't appear to be influenced by the drinking habits of high-profile sportspeople as depicted in the mass media.'

Dr O'Brien and his colleagues, pointing to previous research, suggest that sport and sports stars are much more likely to influence the drinking behaviour of fans when used as marketing tools by the alcohol industry, such as through sponsorship deals.

> **Both sporting and non-sporting study participants believed that sports stars actually drank significantly less than themselves.**

The research team asked more than 1,000 young sportspeople at elite and amateur level and non-sportspeople to report the perceived drinking behaviour of high-profile sports stars compared with their friends. They then had to report their own drinking behaviour using the World Health Organization's Alcohol Use Disorder Identification Test (AUDIT).

The researchers found that both sporting and non-sporting study participants believed that sports stars

He's got a drink problem apparently?

He should be ashamed!

Sports stars are no role models, say scientists

actually drank significantly less than themselves but that their own friends drank considerably more.

After accounting for other potential factors, sports stars' drinking was not predictive of young sportspeople's own drinking, and was actually predictive of lower levels of drinking in non-sportspeople – the more alcohol non-sportspeople perceived sports stars to drink, the less they actually drank themselves.

Young people's own drinking was instead strongly related to the overestimation of their friends' drinking and, in sportspeople only, to sport-specific cultural habits, such as the drinking with competitors after games.

Dr O'Brien added: 'Sport administrators, like the Football Association, are very quick to condemn and punish individual sports stars for acting as poor role models when they are caught displaying drunken and loutish behaviour.

'But there is much stronger evidence for a relationship between alcohol-industry sponsorship, advertising and marketing within sport and dangerous drinking among young people than there is for the influence of sports stars' drinking.

'We are not suggesting that sports stars should not be encouraged to drink responsibly but it's disingenuous to place the blame on them for setting the bad example.

'It is time that sport administrators consider their own social responsibilities when weighing up the costs and benefits of using their sports and sport stars to market alcohol on behalf of the alcohol industry.'

22 April 2010

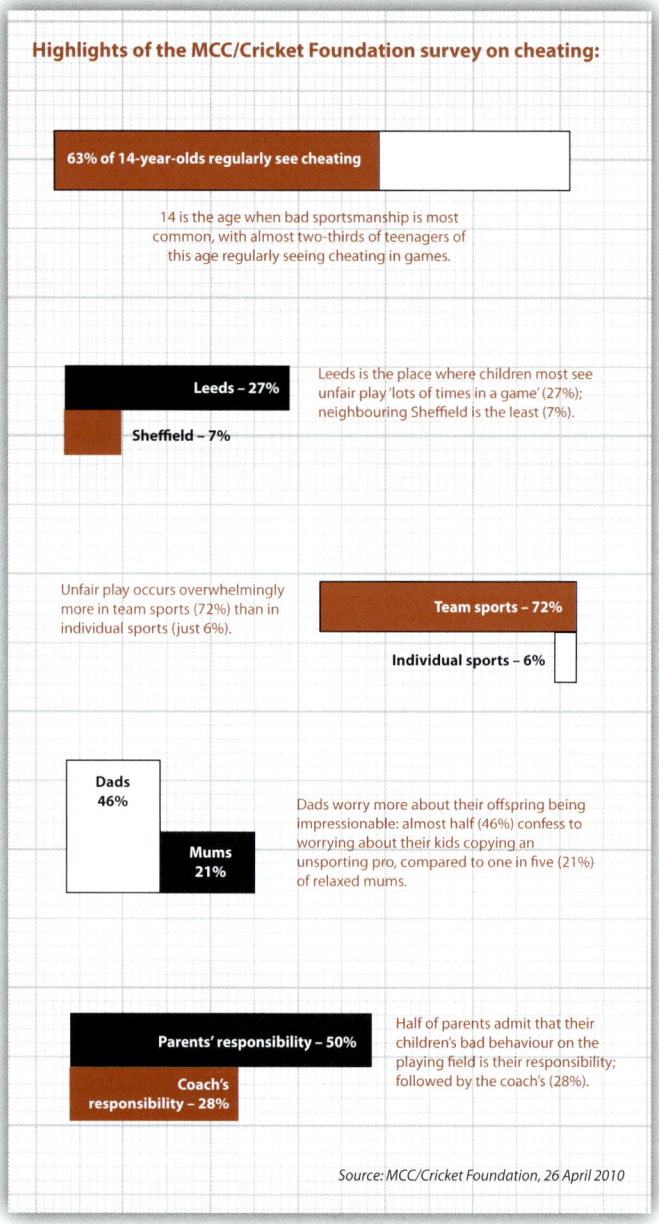

Highlights of the MCC/Cricket Foundation survey on cheating:

63% of 14-year-olds regularly see cheating

14 is the age when bad sportsmanship is most common, with almost two-thirds of teenagers of this age regularly seeing cheating in games.

Leeds – 27%

Sheffield – 7%

Leeds is the place where children most see unfair play 'lots of times in a game' (27%); neighbouring Sheffield is the least (7%).

Unfair play occurs overwhelmingly more in team sports (72%) than in individual sports (just 6%).

Team sports – 72%

Individual sports – 6%

Dads 46%

Mums 21%

Dads worry more about their offspring being impressionable: almost half (46%) confess to worrying about their kids copying an unsporting pro, compared to one in five (21%) of relaxed mums.

Parents' responsibility – 50%

Coach's responsibility – 28%

Half of parents admit that their children's bad behaviour on the playing field is their responsibility; followed by the coach's (28%).

Source: MCC/Cricket Foundation, 26 April 2010

Mini glossary

loutish – *behaving in a drunken and anti-social way*

empirically – *to test with an experiment*

disingenuous – *insincere; untruthful*

" **It is thought that alcohol-industry sponsors and marketing campaigns within sport influence young people's drinking trends.** "

www.manchester.ac.uk

The history of drugs in sport

THE USE OF DRUGS IN SPORT with the aim of improving performance is a major problem for sport's governing bodies. This, however, is not a new phenomenon.

Drugs have been used to enhance performance since ancient times. Greek and Roman civilisations used mushrooms and herbs to improve their performance. Later, in the 19th century, substances including alcohol, opium and caffeine were used.

The more recent forms of performance-enhancing drugs have their roots in World War II, when amphetamines were used by American soldiers to keep them alert and Germans used anabolic steroids to increase their aggressive behaviour. A number of deaths and allegations of drug taking encouraged the International Olympic Committee (IOC) to set up a Medical Commission in 1967 which banned the use of drugs and other performance-enhancing substances. Small-scale testing was introduced at the 1968 Mexico Olympics, followed by a full-scale testing at the next games in Munich, 1972.

In 1975, anabolic steroid use was banned following the development of a test, after which there was an increase in disqualifications through steroid use. In 1983, caffeine and testosterone were added to the prohibited list, followed in 1986 by blood doping and EPO in 1990, despite reliable tests for their detection not being available until 2000.

Following a large number of doping offences being committed in the mid-nineties and the existence of several conflicting organisations, the World Conference on Doping was held in Switzerland in 1999. As a result, the World Anti-Doping Agency (WADA) was formed to promote and co-ordinate the fight against drug use in sport on an international level, across all sports. WADA was set up by the IOC and with the support of other international organisations and governments. The organisation is formed by individuals from the IOC and public authorities.

Why do athletes take drugs?

There are a large number of reasons why an athlete may decide to take drugs. A selection are listed here:

- Pressure to succeed, either from themselves or coaches/family.

- Belief that their competitors are taking drugs.

- Pressure from governments/national authorities (as occurred in the Eastern European countries in the 60s and 70s).

- Financial rewards for outstanding performance.

- Lack of access to, or funding for, training facilities and additional support (nutrition, psychological support).

- Community and media attitudes and expectations of success.

Mini glossary

phenomenon – *a large-scale or extraordinary event*

EPO – *a performance enhancing drug*

The above information is reprinted with kind permission from Teach PE.
© TeachPE.com 2010

www.teachpe.com

Sport cheats are bottom of the class in pupil poll

AS PART OF THE RE-LAUNCH OF MCC SPIRIT OF CRICKET in Chance to Shine schools from today (26 April 2010), The Cricket Foundation and MCC have commissioned a survey on poor sportsmanship, from grassroots to the elite end of sport.

The research finds that professional sportsmen who break the rules are not 'cool for school', and young fans are not as impressionable as we might think.

Three-quarters of 1,015 children aged eight to 16 polled described a sportsperson who does something unfair in a game as a 'cheat' (72%) and 'stupid' (33%); with only four per cent describing them as 'cool'.

Far from being easily influenced, two-thirds of children (67%) say that seeing a famous sportsperson doing something unfair in order to win would not make them more likely to do it themselves.

However, the school playing field is still a hotbed of rule-breaking, with more than half of children (54%) witnessing unfair play in every single game they play. Faking injuries, elbowing in the face, arguing with the umpire and headbutting are among the many examples of gamesmanship that youngsters give in the poll.

Encouragingly, in a like-for-like survey of 200 eight- to 11-year-olds involved in the MCC Spirit of Cricket scheme, the number of children who witness unfair play in every game drops significantly to 37%. Equally, the number of children who say they 'hardly ever' or 'never' see unfair play (41%) is twice that of children who are not part of the fair play scheme (21%).

Mini glossary

impressionable – *easily influenced*

poll – *survey of opinions*

The above information is reprinted with kind permission from Chance to Shine.
© Cricket Foundation Enterprises

www.chancetoshine.org

Highlights of the survey

Other highlights of the MCC/Cricket Foundation national survey include:

▶ 14 is the age when bad sportsmanship is most common, with almost two-thirds (63%) of teenagers of this age regularly seeing cheating in games.

▶ Leeds is the place where children most see unfair play 'lots of times in a game' (27%), neighbouring Sheffield is the least (7%).

▶ Unfair play occurs overwhelmingly more in team sports (72%) than in individual sports (just 6%).

▶ Dads worry more about their offspring being impressionable: almost half (46%) confess to worrying about their kids copying an unsporting pro, compared to one in five (21%) of relaxed mums.

▶ Half of parents admit that their children's bad behaviour on the playing field is their responsibility, followed by the coach's (28%).

Spirit of sport hall of shame

Former boxing champion Mike Tyson's notorious bite on Evander Holyfield's ear in their 1997 heavyweight title match is voted the worst act of bad sportsmanship. Tyson receives a quarter (26%) of parents' votes.

Thierry Henry's double handball against the Republic of Ireland in last year's World Cup qualifier earns him second spot in the 'Spirit of Sport Hall of Shame', surprisingly ahead of Diego Maradona's infamous 'Hand of God' act, which is ranked third.

26 April 2010

Drug testing in sport

DRUG TESTING HAS BECOME AN INCREASINGLY LARGE PART of both professional and amateur sports. An athlete can be called for drug testing at any time, in or out of competition. During competition, some sports only carry out drug testing on the winning team or top three competitors. Others will test by random selection from all competitors.

Urine testing

When called for a drugs test, the athlete is entitled to have a representative (such as their coach or team doctor) present to check that the testing occurred following all guidelines. A urine sample is provided (in view of an official of the same gender) and split into two bottles and sealed by the athlete. A code number will be attached to the bottle and recorded on the relevant paperwork to ensure the correct result is given to the athlete whilst retaining their anonymity.

Following the sampling procedure the athlete must complete a medical declaration which states all medicines, drugs and substances taken over the last week. It is important that the athlete records everything, from over-the-counter medicines to supplements and prescribed drugs. If any of these substances are on the prohibited list the athlete must hold a Therapeutic Use Exemption (TUE) certificate. The competitor, representative and official all check the form before the official and athlete sign it and both parties are given a copy.

The samples are then sent to a registered laboratory (if there is not one on site) where sample A is tested. If a positive result is found with sample A, the athlete is told, then sample B is also tested. The athlete or their representative is entitled to be present at the unsealing and testing of the second sample. If this too is positive, the relevant sporting organisations are told, whose responsibility it is to decide what penalties or bans are to be imposed.

> **The athlete must complete a medical declaration which states all medicines, drugs and substances taken over the last week.**

Blood testing

Blood testing is used in the detection of drugs such as EPO and artificial oxygen carriers by testing the blood count. Over time a 'blood profile' of an athlete can be built up to help determine average readings for each individual. This can help with blood doping tests in the future. The same anonymity and representative procedures apply as for urine sampling.

Again the athlete is asked to select and check the testing and collection equipment before a phlebotomist (an individual trained to draw blood) collects two samples of blood directly into bottles A and B.

The bottles stay in the possession of the athlete (who is always accompanied by an official) until they are sealed in the sample collection kit. Samples are sent to a lab for testing. The same procedure applies as in urine testing, where if the A sample is positive, the B sample is then tested. Another positive result means the appropriate governing bodies are notified.

Mini glossary

anonymity – *keeping someone's identity a secret*

The above information is reprinted with kind permission from Teach PE. © TeachPE.com 2010

www.teachpe.com

Activities

Brainstorm

Brainstorm to find out what you know about sportsmanship.

1. What do you understand by the term 'sportsmanship'?

    ....

    ....

2. How much do professional footballers get paid?

    ....

    ....

3. What illegal drugs are used to enhance sporting ability?

    ....

    ....

    ....

Oral activities

4. Read *A game of two halves: the politics of football* on pages 18-20. In a group, stage a television talk show in which the subject for discussion is 'Should professional footballers be wage capped?'. One member of your group should play the host, one a Premiership footballer, one a League 2 player, one a sports pundit, one a football fan and one the parent of a young fan. Other group members can participate as audience members who submit questions for the panel to consider.

5. Do you enjoy watching or playing a particular sport? How does engaging with this sport make you feel? Why do you prefer it to other sporting activities? Create a presentation entitled 'Why I love [my sport]', and deliver it to your class.

Moral dilemmas

6. During a game of golf, you spot a chance to cheat by nudging your ball with your foot while the other player's back is turned. Would you take this opportunity if you knew there was no chance of being caught? What if you suspected the other player of having cheated but you couldn't prove it – would it then be 'fair' for you to cheat too?

7. Imagine you are a footballer playing for your local League 2 team in the town where you grew up. You have been with the team since you were a youth player and are grateful to them for giving you your start and to the fans for their loyalty. However, one day you are spotted by a talent scout and offered the chance to play for a Premiership team at a much higher salary. Would you take it?

Activities

Research activities

8. Find out about the Scottish skier Alain Baxter, who was stripped of his Bronze medal in the 2002 Winter Olympics after failing a drugs test. Do you think what happened to Baxter was fair? Write a summary of the rules surrounding doping and how they are applied to individual athletes.

   CONCLUSIONS..
   ....
   ....
   ....
   ....

9. Over a week, cut out any newspaper stories you can find about sports stars or their partners which appear OUTSIDE the paper's sports section. Keep these articles in a folder. At the end of the week, review the stories you have collected. Do you think sports stars and their partners are good role models for young people? Do you think they receive too much media attention? Write a summary of your findings.

   NOTES...
   ....
   ....
   ....
   ....

Written activities

Complete the following activities in your exercise books or on a sheet of paper.

10. 'Doping isn't cheating: if all athletes do it, it makes sport fairer. It is just a way for athletes to try and be the best that they can be.' Do you agree with this view at all? Write an essay exploring this view, looking at both sides of the argument and giving your own conclusion.

11. Choose your favourite sport. Write a list of 'The ten rules of good sportsmanship' which you think all players of the sport should follow.

Design activities

12. Find out about some popular doping methods and substances. Choose one and design a poster, discouraging budding sports stars from experimenting with this drug.

Key Facts

- Just over one in five 5- to 19-year-olds (21%) had taken part in three hours or more organised sport outside school in the week prior to interview. 47% had done no organised sport. (page 1)

- Sport England is aiming to have one million more people doing sport by 2013. (page 4)

- London 2012 will make history as the first Games to have representation by men and women in every sport. Men have (to date) been excluded from participating in synchronised swimming. Historically, women have been excluded from boxing. (page 6)

- There is a wide range of sports that people in wheelchairs can play. These include sports such as archery, athletics (track and field), wheelchair basketball, bowls, cue sports (snooker and nine-ball pool), wheelchair rugby, wheelchair racing (road), fencing, handcycling, powerlifting, racquetball, swimming, table tennis and tennis. (page 7)

- There are only seven British Asian players in professional football. (page 10)

- The majority of football fans attending matches have heard homophobic abuse on the terraces. (page 11)

- There were 3,752 arrests related to violence at football grounds during the 2008-09 season – down two per cent on the year before. (page 13)

- A Fabian Society/YouGov survey showed that people in Britain think that a fair average salary for a professional footballer would be £62,000 per year. (page 19)

- The loutish and drunken behaviour of some of our sporting heroes – often reported in the media – has little or no effect on the drinking habits of young people, new research has found. (page 21)

- Drugs have been used to enhance performance since ancient times. Greek and Roman civilisations used mushrooms and herbs to improve their performance. Later, in the 19th century, substances including alcohol, opium and caffeine were used. (page 23)

- 14 is the age when bad sportsmanship is most common, with almost two-thirds (63%) of teenagers of this age regularly seeing cheating in games. (page 24)

- An athlete can be called for drug testing at any time, in or out of competition. During competition, some sports only carry out drug testing on the winning team or top three competitors. Others will test by random selection from all competitors. (page 25)

Glossary

Anabolic steroids – Anabolic steroids are drugs which have the same effect as male reproductive hormones like testosterone. They boost muscle growth, but can also have harmful side effects such as aggression, liver damage and high blood pressure. It is illegal for athletes to take steroids because they can artificially enhance their sporting performance.

Athlete – A highly-trained professional or amateur sportsperson.

Diuretic – A chemical that can be taken by athletes to increase the amount of water expelled from their body when they urinate. This is done to hide banned substances during urine tests, as the urine is more diluted. Diuretic use in sporting competitions is illegal.

Doping – The use of performance-enhancing drugs by athletes during sporting competitions. Most of these are illegal and players have to take a drugs test before taking part in competitive events. If it is found that they have taken drugs they will automatically be disqualified from the event, and may also be banned from taking part in any future competitions for a set period of time.

Hooliganism – A popular term in the past for violence at football matches. Match organisers have worked very hard recently to combat hooliganism. Police presence and other security measures are now routinely put in place to control rioting fans, and repeat 'football hooligans' can be banned from travelling abroad to attend games.

Inclusive sport – Sport which is inclusive does not discriminate on the grounds of gender, ethnicity, sexual orientation or disability. Sport is usually segregated where athletes have a physical difference which makes equal competition difficult – men and women do not usually compete against each other, for example, and nor do disabled and able-bodied athletes. This is called classification. However, there is no ban on any athlete competing in a separate competition. Athletes should be protected from discrimination and unfair treatment, such as racist and homophobic chanting at football matches.

London 2012 – Every four years the Olympic Games are held in a different city around the world. The next Olympics, which will take place in 2012, are to be held in London, Great Britain.

Paralympic Games – The Paralympic Games are a series of sporting competitions open to athletes with physical disabilities. They are held immediately after the Olympic Games. Athletes with disabilities such as amputations, paralysis and blindness take part in a wide range of competitive sports. The next Paralympics will be held in London in 2012.

Stimulant – A drug which causes a temporary improvement in mental or physical functioning.

Wage cap – There is often controversy over the salaries paid to some football players. The highest-paid player in 2010 was Real Madrid's Cristiano Ronaldo, who earned £11.3 million. Some people think it is unfair that footballers should earn such large amounts for playing a sport, far more than professionals such as doctors, and in many cases the salaries paid can nearly bankrupt a club. A wage cap would stop a player earning over a specified amount, or a set percentage of the football club's profits. However, critics say that if this happened in the UK, many of the best football players would move to clubs in other countries.

WAGs – The abbreviation WAGs stands for 'Wives And Girlfriends', and has become a popular label for the partners of footballers. The WAGs are associated with designer clothes and glamorous lifestyles and receive a lot of attention from the media.